MEOW!

ISBN: 978-1-68022-577-8

If Cats Could Talk

new seasons®

Hard day. Hair ball. Nuff said.

If you really want something,
you just have to go in
and get it yourself.

Trust me. It'll be worth the effort.

Half the time I'm not exactly sure how I get up here either.

I am constantly amazed by my friend's complete lack of inhibitions.

Don't try to play cute with me, mister.
I saw you out with the dog.

Jimmy's Fish Market?

Do you deliver?

Hey, these ears
don't scratch themselves.

This may the longest nap
I've ever taken.

I'm going to close my eyes,
and when I open them I hope
there's a feather toy in front of me.

For your sake.

Dog shmog.

How many dogs does it take
to screw in a light bulb?
All of 'em.
One to turn it, and the rest to
run around in circles and bark at it!

Oh, deer!

Then is it good luck if I cross your path?

I <u>told</u> her I had the
whole bath thing covered.

Find your place in the sun. Then take a nap.

Window shade pull string.
Challenge accepted!

I trust my dinner is ready
and waiting for me
in its usual spot.

After a long
day of lying
on the sofa,
I like to unwind
by rolling over
for a stretch
and a nap.

Kitten. Knitten.

If one more person says
"hang in there, baby ..."

I am <u>not</u> a hoppy bunny!

Then you
shouldn't have
put the
dinner rolls
in my
basket.

Your feathery antics are no match
for my feline prowess!

You are getting sleepy.
Your eyelids are getting heavy.
You want to give me a big can of tuna.

I guess this is what she
meant by time out.

I'm sorry that I'm cuter than you.

My. Toys.
Not. Yours.

While I appreciate the
expensive new cat bed, I really
just wanted the box it came in.

I meant to do that!

I know the answer!
The puppy did it!

You missed a spot.

I want to turn over a new leaf...

or eat one,

and I just can't decide which.

I was worshiped by the Egyptians.
There will be no "fetch."

So this is what the other side looks like!

Deep breath in.
Deep breath out.
Now we move into the
Tangled Yarn position.

You want <u>me</u> to try that?
You're hilarious!

I'm having a bad whisker day....

If each day is a gift,
I'd like to know where
I can return Mondays....

Indoor cat, I am an INDOOR cat!

One down,
two to go.

It's funny how you think
I'm listening to you....

Are these <u>my</u> paws?

I wonder why
they called me Boots.

Did I hear the treat container...?
I mean, did you call me?

I put the fur in furniture.

Who is Aunt Karen, and why
does she need a scarf anyway?

MINE!

Any questions?

If I could just figure out
how to turn it on,
I could rule the world.

Are you sure about this?!?

I'm not!

I was supposed to play the princess,
not the pea, in this game.

Time for a nap.
My work here is done.

Photography © Media Bakery, Shutterstock.com, SuperStock, Thinkstock